A World of Sport

An A to Z of Sport

Contents

Gill Howell

RIGBY

Basketball

Two teams of five people play in a basketball match. They throw or bounce the ball to each other. Kicking it is not allowed, but the players can move with the ball. A goal is scored by throwing the ball into a **basket**.

Basketball is popular in the USA and Russia. In the 2004 Olympics, the Americans won the gold medal and the Russians took the bronze.

Russia

USA

Did you know?

Bouncing the ball is called 'dribbling'.

The USA has some of the best basketball players in the world.

Cricket

Cricket is played with a bat, ball and two sets of posts called **wickets**. The **bowler** tries to knock down the wicket behind the batsman. The batsman tries to hit the ball and run to the second wicket near the bowler.

Cricket is one of the most popular sports in England and Pakistan. In 1992, Pakistan won the World Cup when they beat England.

England

Pakistan

A batsmen defends the wicket with a cricket bat.

Did you know?

Cricket balls are made from **cork** and leather.

Football

There are 11 players in a football team.
Players score goals by kicking the ball into a net.
A goalkeeper on each side tries to stop the ball
going into the net. The goalkeeper is the only
player that can use his hands.

*Football is the world's most popular sport. It is played
in over 160 countries. It was probably introduced to
England by the Romans.*

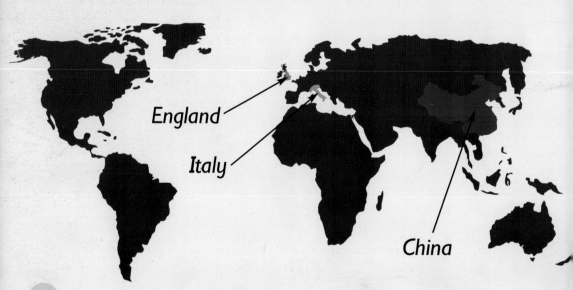

England

Italy

China

Did you know?

Football was played in China over 2000 years ago.

In a football match, the players of each team try to keep the ball.

Hockey

Hockey players use sticks to knock a ball, called a 'puck', into the goal. There are two goal nets on a hockey pitch – one for each side. Each goal counts as one point. There are 11 players in a team. Players wear shin pads to protect their legs.

Hockey is a popular game in India and Pakistan. It has been played for hundreds of years.

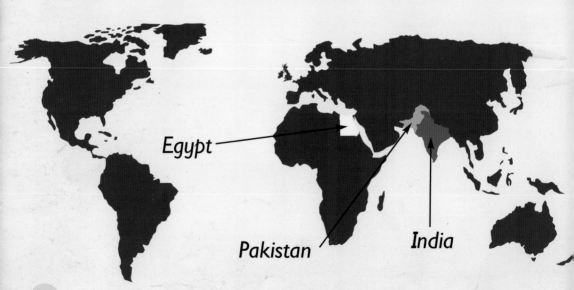

Egypt

Pakistan

India

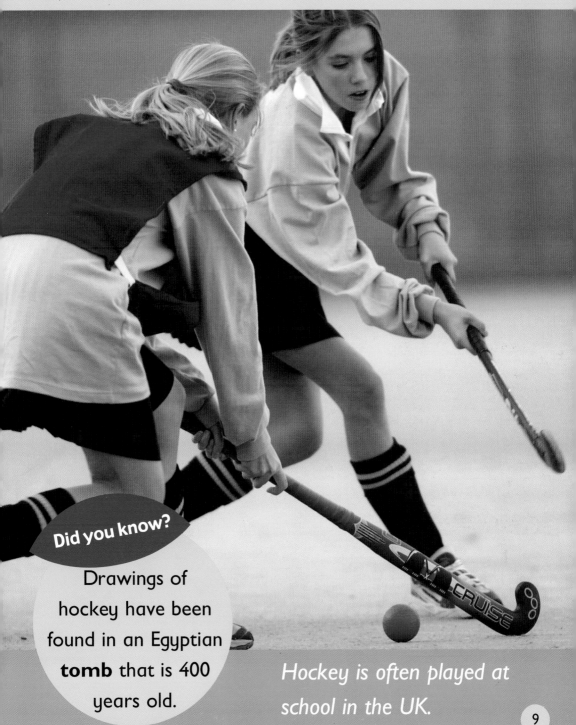

Did you know?

Drawings of hockey have been found in an Egyptian **tomb** that is 400 years old.

Hockey is often played at school in the UK.

Rugby

In rugby, players can throw and kick the ball. They can run with the ball too. Rugby balls are **oval**. Players score points by touching the ground with the ball between two lines. The two lines are found at each end of the pitch.

Many people play rugby in the UK and France. There is a competition between France, England, Scotland, Ireland, Italy and Wales every year.

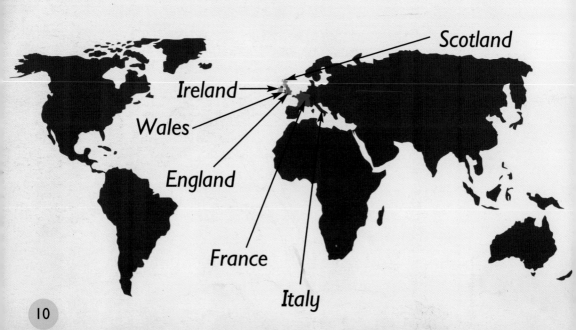

Scotland

Ireland

Wales

England

France

Italy

Did you know?

Rugby was first played at Rugby School in England.

No one can throw the ball forwards in rugby match.

Table Tennis

Table tennis is often called 'ping-pong'. Players hit a small ball over a net on top of a table, using a bat. These bats are sometimes called paddles.

Many people enjoy playing table tennis in China and Brazil. More than 100 countries take part in the world championships.

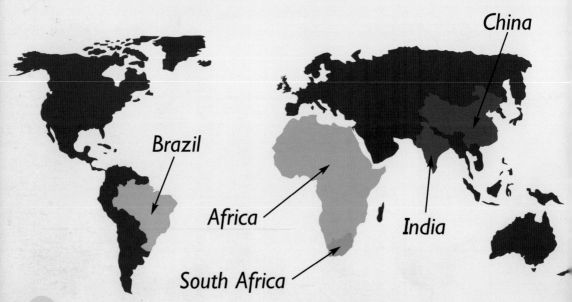

China

Brazil

Africa

India

South Africa

Did you know?

Table tennis was first played by British soldiers in India and South Africa in the 1800s.

Table tennis is a very fast game. Players must move quickly to hit the ball.

Volleyball

There are six players on a volleyball team. Players hit the ball over a high net with their hands. If the ball touches the ground on the other side of the net, the player scores a point. Players hit the ball using either the palm or the top of their hand.

Volleyball is a popular sport in Argentina and Greece.

USA

Greece

Argentina

Did you know?

Volleyball was invented in the the USA 200 years ago.

One team **spikes** the ball over the net. The other team tries to **block** it.

Glossary

basket a hoop with a net used as a goal

bowler a player who tosses or bowls the ball to the batter

block when a player stops the ball from going over the net

cork the bark of a special type of oak tree

oval egg-shaped

spike to punch the ball downwards over the net

tomb a burial place

wicket three posts (stumps) and two bails like a small gate

Index